ANIMALS

Modern Publishing

A Division of Unisystems, Inc.

New York, New York 10022

CONTENTS

Animals In Their Environments

Adaptation—All animals and plants are perfectly adapted to their environments. As environments change, living things must adapt or else they do not survive. Over millions of years species have adapted, evolving a little at a time to their surroundings and food supply. In each generation, individuals that have adapted are more able to survive and their young are more likely to survive as well.

Predators and Prey

Big, Fast, and Tall—Most animals are either meat eaters (carnivores) or plant eaters (herbivores). Lions, leopards, and cheetahs are carnivores. Elephants, bucks, zebras, and wildebeests are herbivores. Carnivores eat herbivores. For protection, herbivores have developed in special ways. Some, like elephants and rhinoceroses, are very big. Some, like zebras and bucks, are able to run very fast. Some, like giraffes, are tall and able to see their predators from far away.

An Ocean of Sand

African Desert—
The dromedary is a camel with one hump. It lives in north Africa where it is very hot and almost never rains. Dromedaries and camels are the animals best known for adapting to life in the desert. They store food in their humps in the form of fat. This enables them to go for long periods without eating or drinking. They have broad hooves that do not sink into the soft sand and are good for walking long distances. Their eyes are protected by very long lashes. During sandstorms they can even close their noses using special muscles. Beneath the hot sands and rock there is water. Sometimes it surfaces and forms a pond, called an "oasis," where acacia and date palm trees grow. Elsewhere in the desert very few plants or grasses grow.

1 - wheatear   2 - Sahara sparrows   3 - dromedary   4 - fennec fox
5 - spiny tailed agama   6 and 9 - jerboa   7 - dorcas gazelle
8 - scorpion   10 - addax   11 - sidewinder   12 - giant centipede

From Rock to Rock

High in the Mountains—When you are in the mountains stop and watch quietly. See how many different little animals you can see. Way above, eagles soar and sometimes dive down to capture a woodchuck or another small animal. Many unusual animals live in the mountains. They climb the rocks with ease. Mountain goats are very sure-footed. They have no trouble jumping from rock to rock without slipping. Their hooves are small and strong and well adapted to landing on the steep rocks. High in the mountains there are no trees but there are bushes and beautiful wildflowers growing among the rocks.

1 - Rocky Mountain goat   2 - bighorn sheep   3 - grizzly bear
4 - wolverine   5 - woodchuck   6 - mountain pika   7 - partridge
8 - golden eagle

Watch Out for the Cactus

North American Desert—There is not much water in the American desert. What little there is stays underground and is absorbed by the plants that live in the harsh environment. Animals that live in the desert get their water by eating the plants, and they have learned how to avoid the spines on the cactuses. Plants that live in the desert are used as homes by some of the desert animals. Some animals, like the lynx, will climb to the top of a large cactus to escape from a predator.

1 - bobcat 2 - elf owl 3 - skunk 4 - peccary 5 - badger 6 - fox
7 - Gila monster 8 - desert tortoise 9 - rat 10 - horned lizard
11 - sidewinder 12 - kangaroo rat 13 - roadrunner

The Land of the Cowboys

American Prairie—Once the American prairie was covered with a sea of grass. Now most of the land has been cultivated and is filled with fields of wheat and corn. But wild animals still roam the prairie. Coyotes still howl and hunt prairie dogs. Prairie dogs are rodents that live underground in dens with long tunnels that connect to form underground "cities." Prairie dogs are very watchful. One always stands guard at the entrance to a den. If danger is near, the "watchdog" will make a loud whistle to warn the other prairie dogs. They are very hard to surprise.

1 - bison   2 - pronghorns   3 - coyote   4 - prairie dogs
5 - burrowing owl   6 - sage grouse   7 - horned larks
8 - ground squirrel   9 - rattlesnake

Who Owns the Land?

Who Owns the Prairie?—Buffaloes once roamed the prairie in numbers too large to count. Their only enemies were bears and Native Americans who hunted them for their meat and skins. When the early pioneers arrived they wanted land for farming, and millions of buffaloes were killed without any thought. Land where buffaloes once roamed is now covered with roads and railways and towns. At one time the buffaloes were almost extinct but now their numbers have increased in farms, zoos, and reserves.

WHERE IN THE WORLD DO ANIMALS LIVE?

European
Forest

EUROPE

African Desert

AFRICA

African
Forest

African Savanna

SOUTH POLE

Canadian
Forest

NORTH AMERICA

American
Forest

American
Desert

American
Prairie

American
Swamp

Amazon Forest

SOUTH AMERICA

Grizzly Bear
North America

Monkeys
African Savanna
and Forests

Seals
Polar Regions

Wild Goat
European and
Asian Mountains

Fox
Europe and Asia

Tiger
Asian Jungle

Weasel
Europe and the
Americas

Reindeer
Tundra

Koala
Australian Forests

Horses
Throughout
the world

Camel
Africa and Asia

Kangaroo
Australian Bush

Open and look for a ship that travels under water.

Zebra
African Savanna

Walruses
Polar Regions

Elephant
African Savanna

Penguins
Antarctic

Giraffe
African Savanna

Wolf
Europe and North America

Ostrich
African Savanna

Buffalo
North American Prairie

It is a submarine with a periscope.

Dromedaries
North African Desert

Lynx
American Desert

AUSTRALIA

Australian
Bush

NORTH POLE

Tundra

ASIA

Asian Desert

Asian Jungle

What Makes an Environment?

Every environment is home for the plants and animals that live there. We know how a house is built, and we are learning how an environment is created. Sunlight makes plants grow. Herbivores, birds, and insects eat plants. Carnivores eat the herbivores. Plants, animals, and insects that die (as well as animal droppings) fertilize the earth so new plants can grow. Then the whole cycle begins again. When you look at any environment you will see that things are always growing and dying. Our planet earth is one very large environment made up of hundreds of thousands of small environments, all inter-connected and interdependent, like a giant puzzle.

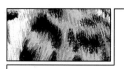

The Importance of Color

Camouflage—Besides being very beautiful, a tiger's striped fur is also very useful. The colors black, white, and orange make a tiger "disappear" in the dappled shade of a tropical jungle. This is called "camouflage." Being able to hide is very important for all animals, whether they are hunting or being hunted. Some animals, such as the weasel, even change colors completely to match their environment as the seasons change. The weasel becomes white in winter to blend in with the snow. The chameleon becomes the color of whatever it is standing on. Camouflage helps animals escape from predators in their environment.

Where the Kangaroos Hop

Australian Bush—Kangaroos are native to Australia and it is the only place they live. The mother kangaroo has a pocket of skin on her stomach, called a "pouch," where the baby kangaroo nurses and grows until it is able to take care of itself. A baby kangaroo is called a "joey." All animals that have a pouch in which their babies develop and grow are called "marsupials." Another Australian marsupial is the koala bear. Among the strangest Australian mammals is the duck-billed platypus, which lays eggs like a reptile but nurses its young like a mammal.

1 - great glider   2 - sugar glider   3 - emu   4 - cuscus
5 - Tasmanian wolf   6 - wallaby   7 - lorikeet   8 - koala
9 - kangaroo   10 - lace monitor   11 - Australian echidna
12 - duckbilled platypus   13 - cassowary

Giraffes and Their Friends

Savanna—The savanna is the great African prairie. It is covered with grasslands: green in the rainy season and yellow in the dry season. Here and there grow large baobab trees—whose large trunks are filled with water—and thorny acacia trees. Giraffes eat the leaves at the tops of the acacias. The thorns don't bother them because their lips and tongues are covered with thick skin. It is hard for animals to hide in the savanna. For protection, animals like antelopes, zebras, giraffes, and bucks are able to run very fast to escape from predators. Predators are animals like lions, leopards, and cheetahs that kill and eat other animals. Jackals and hyenas are also predators but they, like vultures, are scavengers. They eat the remains of animals that have been killed by predators, or they eat animals that have died of old age or by accident.

1 - lions   2 - cheetah   3 - elephants   4 - giraffes   5 - zebras
6 and 7 - antelopes   8 - ostriches   9 - vultures

At Home in a River

The River—What a leap! Frogs are not the only ones that can leap and dive for their dinner. Trout dart out of the water and catch insects that skim along the surface. They are at home in cold mountain streams, in rivers in the warmer plains, and in lakes. To lay their eggs, or "spawn," trout travel upstream against the current. When the young hatch, they travel back downstream to rivers and lakes. Trout are very particular about where they live. They cannot live in polluted rivers full of algae that use up most of the oxygen.

1 - mayfly   2 - dragonfly   3 - European tree frog   4 - snipe   5 - mallard duck
6 - common frog   7 - carp   8 - scavenger beetle   9 - mayfly larva   10 - tench
11 - dragonfly larva   12 - whirligig beetles   13 - great diving beetle
14 - grass snake   15 - white stork   16 - tadpoles   17 - great diving beetle larva
18 - warty newt larva   19 - water snail   20 - warty newt   21 - bittern

Where the Salmon Live

Canadian Forest—Salmon swim from the sea back upriver to where they were born. With great leaps, they navigate up waterfalls and log dams that beavers build in the rapids. Bears wade into the rivers to scoop up a tasty meal of salmon, but often they are content to eat honey or wild berries. Bears often move very slowly, but if necessary, they can run very fast. They can easily catch a deer but usually prefer to attack when the animal is tired or wounded. Among the thick fir trees, the larch trees, and the white birch trees of Canada, winter comes very early. At the first sign of snow, bears find a den. There they hibernate through the cold winter months. In the spring female bears often emerge with cubs that have been born during the winter. The cubs stay warm by pressing close to their mother's fur.

1 - American moose   2 - wolf   3 - Canadian lynx
4 - beavers   5 - otter   6 - raccoons   7 - porcupine
8 - elk 9 - American black bears   10 - salmon

Among the Birch Trees

American Forest—The opossum is the only North American marsupial. Female marsupials have a pouch on their stomachs where their babies develop and grow. When the babies are old enough to crawl out of the pouch, the mother carries them on her back. Opossums, like owls, hunt at night. When opossums are threatened, they lie absolutely still and pretend they are dead so their enemies will leave them alone. Opossums have to beware of gray foxes that eat small animals like opossums, squirrels, and cottontail rabbits.

1 - opossums   2 - flying squirrel   3 - eastern hairy woodpecker
4 - yellow-shafted flicker   5 - cardinal   6 - gray fox
7 - white-tailed deer   8 - eastern box turtle   9 - striped skunk
10 - deer mouse   11 - wild turkey   12 - eastern cottontail

Life in a Swamp

American Swamp—On the swampy coasts of Florida, mangrove trees grow. Many kinds of animals, snakes, and birds live there. Alligators spend their time catching fish or sunning themselves on the banks of the rivers. They are slow on land but they are very fast in the water. Female alligators make a nest by digging a hole in the mud and filling it with rotting grasses to keep the eggs warm. When the eggs hatch the mother recognizes her babies by their cries, which are similar to a frog's croaks. Snapping turtles, lizards, and very colorful birds, like the roseate spoonbill, the green heron, and the brown pelican, are at home in the swamp.

1 - roseate spoonbills   2 - green heron   3 - limpkin   4 - water moccasin
5 - brown pelican   6 - bald eagle   7 - alligator   8 - gar pikes
9 - purple gallinule   10 - American egrets   11 - wood ibis   12 - snakebird
13 - common snapper turtle   14 - white ibises   15 - Virginian deer

On the Banks of the Great River

Amazon Forest—Tapirs live in the forest along the Amazon River—the second longest river in the world. Their many enemies, the jaguar, a silent, efficient hunter; the anaconda snake, which wraps around its prey and squeezes it to death; and the black caiman, a crocodile that hunts at night, all hide in the dense growth of the forest. In the river swim piranha, small fish capable of devouring a large animal in just a few minutes. The Amazon forest is hot and very humid, like a greenhouse. That is why more kinds of plants grow there than anywhere else in the world—including rubber trees and orchids, which send down roots into other plants.

1 - umbrella bird   2 - ruffled marmoset   3 - capuchin   4 - brown capuchin
5 - white-fronted marmoset   6 - two-toed sloth   7 - red and green macaw
8 - giant anaconda   9 - giant otter   10 - white-lipped peccary
11 - common opossum   12 - jaguar   13 - South American tapirs
14 - rainbow boa   15 - toucan   16 - Amazon ants

A Green Labyrinth

African Forest—Leopards love to climb trees. It is difficult to see them up high because their spotted fur blends with the vegetation (camouflage). In one leap they can surprise their prey. Leopards can creep quietly through the hot equatorial forest that is filled with the noises of other animals. Monkeys howl, colorful birds shriek, wild pigs snort, and snakes hiss. Vines hang from the trees and the ground is covered with ferns and bright flowers. The trees grow so close together they get tangled up and very little light can get through.

1 - leopard   2 - duiker   3 - serval   4 - okapis   5 - drana monkeys
6 - hornbill   7 - pangolin   8 - hamadryad baboons   9 - bush pigs
10 - gorillas   11 - black mamba   12 - python

A Thousand Eyes Behind the Leaves

Asian Jungle—Proboscis monkeys live on the island of Borneo in the Malay Archipelago, which is in Asia. Their noses are very unusual. The male can make his nose swell up to attract females. Proboscis monkeys live in the jungle, which is filled with tall trees, flowering bushes, vines, and plants with roots in water. The monkeys live in the trees and can cross the whole forest without touching the ground, by jumping from tree to tree! They can jump as far as 20 feet. Proboscis monkeys eat fruits and insects that they find in the trees. Their enemies are cobras, pythons, and leopards (which in the jungle can be completely black).

1 - gray gibbon   2 - proboscis monkey   3 - western tarsier
4 - Indian rock python   5 - squacco heron   6 - king cobra   7 - grebe
8 - adjutant stork   9 - painted stork   10 - crocodile   11 - mallard duck
12 - water viper   13 - pheasant-tailed jacana   14 - archer fish
15 - mandarin ducks   16 - clarius catfish   17 - frog   18 - purple swamp hen

Ice, Moss, and Lichen

Tundra—The tundra is covered with snow for most of the year. When the snow melts, the lichens appear. They are made up of tiny green plants and fungi. Moss also starts to grow. It is bright green and spongy with water. In the two summer months grasses and colorful flowers sprout. There are no tall trees on the tundra because the roots cannot get through the ground,which is always frozen deep down. Snowy owls live on the tundra. Unlike other birds, owls' eyes are in the front of their heads instead of on the sides. Owls can see depths and distances very well. When they are flying high, this helps them spot their prey such as lemmings. Lemmings are small rodents that dig long tunnels underground.

1 - long-tailed jaegers   2 - snowy owl   3 - willow ptarmigan   4 - caribou
5 - wolf   6 - arctic fox   7 - musk oxen   8 - Canada geese
9 - red-breasted merganser   10 - arctic loon   11 - arctic hares
12 - lemmings   13 - snow bunting   14 - old squaws   15 - grayling

Glossary

archipelago—a large body of water with many islands.

carnivore—an animal that eats meat.

deciduous—a plant that loses its leaves once a year.

desert—an area that has little or no rainfall and very few plants grow there.

ecology—the science that studies environments.

environment—all the conditions including plants, animals, and climate that affect a living thing.

equatorial—having to do with the equator, an imaginary line running from west to east that cuts the earth in half.

evergreen—a plant that does not shed its leaves or needles each year.

evolution—the process by which a plant or animal species changes to survive over time.

extinct—when there are no more living individuals of a particular species.

fertilize—to make productive.

forest—an area of land where lots of trees grow.

fungus—a plant without roots or leaves that cannot make its own food. It absorbs nutrients by living on other plants or animals.

greenhouse—a building for growing plants, usually made of glass. A green-house is usually warm and humid.

habitat—the natural home of an animal or plant.

herbivore—an animal that eats plants.

hibernate—to spend the winter sleeping, often in a den or burrow.

jungle—an area of land that is densely covered with plants and trees. Jungles are either tropical or rain forest.

litter—a group of young animals born at the same time to the same mother.

mangrove—a kind of tree that grows in swamps and forms new land masses by sending down roots and multiplying.

marsupial—an animal that carries its young in a pouch where they grow and develop.

migrate—to move from one habitat to another. Some birds, animals, and fish migrate to different climates or feeding grounds as the seasons change.

navigate—to direct or plan which way to travel.

nocturnal—an animal that is active at night.

omnivore—an animal that eats plants and animals.

permafrost—the lower levels of soil in the arctic regions that are frozen all year round.

photosynthesis—the process by which plants turn sunlight into living plant matter. A plant captures the energy of the sun through its leaves and combines it with water vapor and carbon dioxide from the air to make food. Without sunlight, plants cannot make food.

predator—an animal that kills other animals for its food.

rain forest—an area covered with tall evergreen trees where there is an exceptionally high rainfall.

rodent— an animal like a squirrel, mouse, or rat, that gnaws and nibbles.

savanna—an area of land covered with grass that has rainfall during certain seasons.

scavenger—an animal that eats the flesh of animals that have died or been killed by other animals.

silt—the fine sand and tiny rock particles at the bottom of rivers.

species—a group of animals or plants that are very similar to each other and can breed with each other. They produce offspring that can reproduce as well.

swamp—land that is very wet, spongy, and full of plants.

tundra—a very cold area of land in the northern hemisphere where the ground is frozen most of the year.

Concept by Elisabetta Dami, Anna Casalis, Francesca Grazzini, Adriana Sirena

U.S. edition designed by Barbara Lipp

U.S. text by Debby Slier

Illustrated by G. B. Bertelli, Piero Cattaneo, Alessandra Cimatoribus, Enzio Giglioli,
Matteo Lupatelli, Rosalba Moriggia, Maria Piatto, Rudolf Sablic

Printed in EEC, Officine Grafiche De Agostini - Novara 1994
Bound by Legatoria del Verbano S.p.A.